DO ONE THING EVERY DAY TO MAKE YOU SMILE

A Journal by

Improving our world,
one smile at a time.

World Smile Foundation

If the slogan of the World Smile Foundation seems like a grand aim for a modest facial expression, consider the words quoted in this journal. Philosophers, artists, novelists, poets, musicians, athletes, celebrities, and (of course) comics all attest to the power of a smile. "A smile is the same as sunshine; it banishes winter from the human countenance" (Victor Hugo). "That smile could end wars and cure cancer" (John Green). "Every smile makes you a day younger" (Chinese proverb). And from Marilyn Monroe, who had her own classic smile: "A smile is the best makeup any girl can wear."

On almost every page of *Do One Thing Every Day to Make You Smile*, you can either experience a smile in the moment or recall and record a smile you want to save to brighten a dark time. Flip through the pages each day to find one that feels right, fill in the blank dateline, and prepare to smile. You may be asked to respond to a quotation or illustration with words or a drawing of your own; to list your lifelong sources of smiles in categories such as food, film, sports, and music; or to note the spark of a small private smile that day (a flower, freebie, surprise, nap, even fresh sheets, for example). Enjoy the jokes of famous comedians, record your own, then try out both. On pages of Wordplay, discover absurd names of real places; smile at malapropisms, misprints, muddled translations of film titles, and wild definitions of words, real and imaginary, from the past and present.

We hope that you will smile as much as we did as you read through this book. Scientists have shown that smiling itself has the power to make you happy by activating circuitry in your brain that produces feel-good hormones. And since "most smiles are started by another smile" (Frank Howard Clark), you can set off a chain reaction—which should make your smile even wider.

DATE: __ / __ / __

According to research studies, the average adult smiles 20 times a day, while the average *happy* adult smiles 40 to 50 times. Keep track of your smiles today. Then, after 365 days of *Do One Thing Every Day to Make You Smile*, repeat this smile count at the end of the book and compare.

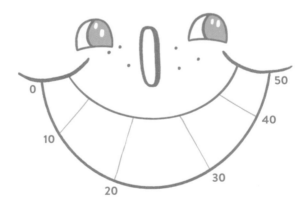

A SMILE IS A CURVE THAT SETS EVERYTHING STRAIGHT.

Phyllis Diller

A smile from _____ set everything straight today.

The smile is the shortest distance between two persons.

Victor Borge

A smile connected me with this friend today:

_____

_____

_____

_____

_____

FILMS
that always *make me*
SMILE

1.

2.

3.

4.

5.

6.

7.

8.

All women love Colin Firth: Mr. Darcy, Mark Darcy, George VI—at this point he could play the Craigslist Killer and people would be like, "Oh my God, the Craigslist Killer has the most boyish smile!"

Mindy Kaling

Actor/actress who always makes me smile:

_____

_____

_____

_____

_____

Always wear a smile, because your smile is a reason for many others to smile.

A.A. Milne

I saw _____ 's smile today and it made me smile, too.

If she but smile, the crystal calm shall break

In music, sweeter than it ever gave,

As when a breeze breathes o'er some
sleeping lake,

And laughs in every wave.

Bayard Taylor

Describe how the most awesome smile affects you:

If _____ but smile, I feel like _____

_____

THINK OF SOMETHING
WONDERFUL
SOMETHING TO
SHOUT ABOUT
MENTION SOMETHING
BEAUTIFUL
SMILES ARE
FROM INSIDE OUT.

Fred Rogers

Copyright © 2023 by ROBIE LLC
Conceived and compiled by Dian G. Smith and Robie Rogge.
All rights reserved.

Published in the United States by Clarkson Potter/Publishers, an imprint of the
Crown Publishing group, a division of Penguin Random House LLC, New York.
ClarksonPotter.com

CLARKSON POTTER is a trademark and POTTER with colophon is a registered
trademark of Penguin Random House LLC.

ISBN 978-0-593-57970-1

Printed in China

Editor: Deanne Katz
Designer: Annalisa Sheldahl
Production Editor: Joyce Wong
Production Manager: Luisa Francavilla
Compositors: DIX Type and Nick Patton
Copy Editor: Drew Wheeler
Marketer: Chloe Aryeh

Book and cover design by Annalisa Sheldahl

10 9 8 7 6 5 4 3 2 1

First Edition

DATE: ___/___/___

I am beginning to measure myself in strength, not pounds. Sometimes in smiles.

Laurie Halse Anderson

After a year of *Do One Thing Every Day To Make You Smile*, count your smiles today and record them here. Then compare this smile chart to the one at the beginning of the book.

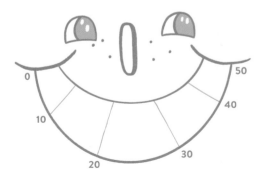

DATE: ___ / ___ / ___

Wake up with a smile and go after life. . . . Live it, enjoy it, taste it, smell it, feel it.

Joe Kapp

I went after life with my smile today. What happened:

_____

_____

_____

_____

_____

_____

_____

Laughter is day, and sobriety is night; a smile is the twilight that hovers gently between both, more bewitching than either.

Henry Ward Beecher

The most bewitching smile today:

_____

_____

_____

_____

_____

NEVER REGRET ANYTHING THAT MADE YOU SMILE.

Unknown

I will never regret ☐ seeing ☐ hearing ☐ doing this today, which made me smile:

_____

_____

_____

_____

DATE: ___/___/___

WHY I SMILED AT BREAKFAST:

_____

_____

_____

DATE: ___/___/___

WHY I SMILED AT LUNCH:

_____

_____

_____

DATE: ___/___/___

WHY I SMILED AT SUPPER:

_____

_____

_____

He smiled rather too much. He smiled at breakfast, you know.

Charles Wheeler

COMMON SENSE AND A SENSE OF HUMOR ARE THE SAME THING, MOVING AT DIFFERENT SPEEDS. A SENSE OF HUMOR IS JUST COMMON SENSE, DANCING.

Clive James

Give an example of common sense dancing:

_____

_____

_____

_____

_____

DATE: ___/___/___

WIT MAKES YU THINK, HUMOR MAKES YOU LAFF.

Josh Billings

Give an example of wit from today that also made you laugh:

_____

_____

_____

_____

_____

THE WORLD IS SO FULL OF A NUMBER OF THINGS,

I'M SURE WE SHOULD ALL BE AS HAPPY AS KINGS.

Robert Louis Stevenson

A possession that made me feel royally happy today:

_____

_____

_____

_____

_____

OBJECTS
that always   make me
SMILE

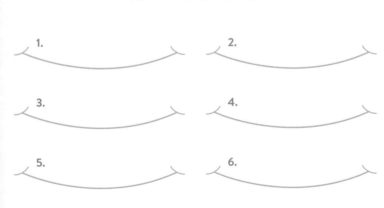

1.

2.

3.

4.

5.

6.

7.

8.

If you help others with sincere motivation and sincere concern, that will bring you more fortune, more friends, more smiles, and more success.

14th Dalai Lama

How I earned more smiles today:

_____

_____

_____

_____

_____

A GENTLE WORD, A KIND LOOK, A GOOD-NATURED SMILE CAN WORK WONDERS AND ACCOMPLISH MIRACLES.

William Hazlitt

A miracle my smile accomplished today:

_____

_____

_____

_____

_____

A Scout smiles and whistles under all circumstances. . . . It cheers him and cheers other people, especially in time of danger.

Robert Baden-Powell

DATE: ___/___/___

MY ☐ SMILING ☐ WHISTLING CHEERED ME UP TODAY WHEN:

_____

_____

_____

_____

_____

_____

DATE: ___/___/___

MY ☐ SMILING ☐ WHISTLING CHEERED UP OTHERS TODAY WHEN:

_____

_____

_____

_____

_____

_____

Humor is a serious thing. I like to think of it as one of our greatest and earliest natural resources which should be preserved at all costs.

James Thurber

How I used humor to resolve a disagreement today:

_____

_____

_____

_____

_____

DATE: ___ / ___ / ___

HUMOR VERY OFTEN CUTS THE KNOT OF SERIOUS QUESTIONS MORE TRENCHANTLY AND SUCCESSFULLY THAN SEVERITY.

Horace

How I used humor to solve a serious problem today:

_____

_____

_____

_____

_____

Human felicity is produced not so much by the great pieces of good fortune that seldom happen, as by little advantages that occur every day.

Benjamin Franklin

A little advantage that made me smile today:

_____

_____

_____

_____

_____

DATE: ___/___/___

WHAT MADE ME SMILE TODAY · WHAT MADE ME SMILE TODA

Complete one or more prompts:

Good weather:_____

Blast from the past:_____

This treat to eat: _____

Afternoon nap:_____

Hugs from: _____

Finding money: _____

Smile from:_____

Other:_____

DATE: ___/___/___

I believe that laughing is the best calorie burner.

Audrey Hepburn

Today I laughed away the calories in a ☐ carrot ☐ candy bar ☐ pizza

☐ steak ☐ _____
other

NEGATIVITY ISN'T THE WAY TO GO, SMILE MORE, EAT SOME CHOCOLATE.

Ed Sheeran

Today I smiled more because I ate some _____.

DATE: __ / __ / __

A FUNNY WORD THAT MADE ME SMILE TODAY:

DATE: __ / __ / __

A FUNNY NOISE THAT MADE ME SMILE TODAY:

BREVITY IS THE SOUL OF WIT.

William Shakespeare

GO FORWARD IN LIFE WITH A TWINKLE IN YOUR EYE AND A SMILE ON YOUR FACE, BUT WITH GREAT AND STRONG PURPOSE IN YOUR HEART.

Gordon B. Hinckley

What I accomplished with a smile and purpose today:

_____

_____

_____

_____

_____

What sunshine is to flowers, smiles are to humanity. These are but trifles, to be sure; but scattered along life's pathway, the good they do is inconceivable.

Joseph Addison

Some good my trifling smile did today:

_____

_____

_____

_____

_____

COLIN IS THE SORT OF NAME YOU GIVE YOUR GOLDFISH FOR A JOKE.

Colin Firth

_____ is the sort of name you give your

your name

_____ for a joke.

WORDPLAY

Boys' Names

What could you name your son to make people smile? Match the columns. (See answers below.)

. . . if your last name is Hurt? _____

. . . if your last name is Register? _____

. . . if your last name is Powder? _____

. . . if your last name is McFall? _____

. . . if your last name is Bacon? _____

1. Macon

2. Trip

3. Kash

4. Will

5. Malcolm

DATE: ___/___/___

SMILE IS A GOOD REPLY TO THE DARK WORLD.

Mehmet Murat Ildan

I used my smile to lighten this darkness today:

_____

_____

_____

_____

_____

The world is like a mirror; if you smile at it, it smiles at you.

Peace Pilgrim

When my smile was mirrored today:

_____

_____

_____

_____

_____

She wore a fixed smile that wa'nt a smile; there wa'nt no light behind it, same's a lamp can't shine if it ain't lit.

Willa Cather

DATE: ___/___/___

WHO LIT MY SMILE TODAY:

_____

_____

_____

_____

_____

_____

DATE: ___/___/___

WHAT LIT MY SMILE TODAY:

_____

_____

_____

_____

_____

_____

DATE: ___/___/___

I COMMENDED MIRTH.

Bible (Ecclesiastes)

Smiling at _____ felt divine today:

_____

_____

_____

_____

_____

Even the gods love their jokes.

Plato

A divine joke someone told me today:

_____

_____

_____

_____

_____

Pick a smiley face that reflects your day. Explain why.

_____

_____

_____

_____

_____

Pick a smiley face that reflects your day. Explain why.

_____

_____

_____

_____

_____

Humor is emotional chaos remembered in tranquility.

James Thurber

An emotionally chaotic moment from the past that made me smile today:

_____

_____

_____

_____

_____

DATE: ___ / ___ / ___

A happy moment can last a lifetime if you remember to smile when you think of it.

Unknown

A happy moment from the past that made me smile today:

_____

_____

_____

_____

_____

DATE: ___ / ___ / ___

HOW I PUT A SMILE ON _____ 'S FACE TODAY:

_____

_____

_____

_____

_____

_____

DATE: ___ / ___ / ___

HOW A SMILE I GAVE CAME BACK TO ME TODAY:

_____

_____

_____

_____

_____

_____

If you put a smile on people's faces, they give that back to you.

Heidi Klum

THE IRISH SENSE OF HUMOR IS SAID TO BE A MAN KISSES THE BLARNEY STONE, THEN FALLS AND FRACTURES HIS SKULL.

John Gregory Dunne

A bit of physical comedy that made me smile today:

_____

_____

_____

_____

_____

**When Irish eyes are smiling,
Sure, 'tis like the morn in spring
In the lilt of Irish laughter
You can hear the angels sing.**

Chauncey Olcott

When _____ eyes are smiling, sure, 'tis like:

_____

_____

_____

_____

_____

DATE: __ / __ / __

YOU CANNOT LOOK AT A SLEEPING CAT AND FEEL TENSE.

Jane Pauley

Today I looked at a ☐ cat ☐ dog ☐ giraffe ☐ goldfish

☐ _____ and calmly smiled.
        other

ANIMALS
that always   make me
SMILE

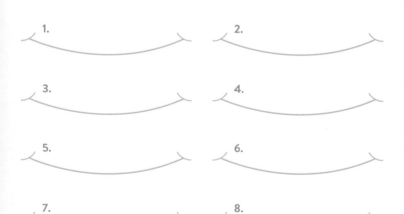

1.

2.

3.

4.

5.

6.

7.

8.

BETTER THE LAST SMILE THAN THE FIRST LAUGHTER.

Proverb

I had the last smile on this matter today:

_____

_____

_____

_____

Ha!

DATE: ___ /___ /___

Remember even though the outside world might be raining, if you keep on smiling the sun will soon show its face and smile back at you.

Anna Lee

Smiling through this personal rainstorm brought out the sun today:

_____

_____

_____

_____

_____

A tender smile,
our sorrows'
only balm.

Edward Young

DATE: ___/___/___

A SMILE FROM _____ THAT SOOTHED ME TODAY:

_____

_____

_____

_____

_____

_____

DATE: ___/___/___

A SMILE FROM ME THAT SOOTHED _____ TODAY:

_____

_____

_____

_____

_____

_____

That was the first time I ever saw him smile. It transformed him from someone menacing to someone you wished you knew.

Suzanne Collins

A smile transformed _____
name

from _____ to _____ .

DATE: ___ / ___ / ___

To someone who has seen a dozen people frown, scowl or turn their faces away, your smile is like the sun breaking through the clouds.

Dale Carnegie

I received this compliment on my smile today:

_____

_____

_____

_____

_____

DATE: ___ /___ /___

THIS IS A TERRIBLE, TERRIBLE SECRET. I'M ALWAYS THINKING OF THE JOKE. YOU ARE A THOUGHT MACHINE. EVERYTHING YOU SEE, HEAR, EXPERIENCE IS USABLE.

Steve Martin

Something I ☐ saw   ☐ heard   ☐ experienced   today that I could use in a joke:

_____

_____

_____

_____

COMICS'
FAVORITE
JOKES

chaha

STEVE
MARTIN

" Tom Lehrer influenced me with one bizarre joke
about an individualist friend whose name was Henry,
only to give you an idea of what an individualist he
was, he spelled it H-E-N-3-R-Y. "

A bizarre joke about my individualist friend _____:

_____

_____

_____

You can shed tears that she is gone or you can smile because she has lived.

David Harkins

I smiled today at this happy memory of someone who is gone:

_____

_____

_____

_____

_____

DATE: ___ / ___ / ___

A SMILE HAPPENS IN A FLASH, BUT ITS MEMORY CAN LAST A LIFETIME.

Bertrand Russell

I smiled today at this happy memory:

_____

_____

_____

_____

_____

DATE: ___/___/___

THIS JOY WAS THE SOURCE OF MY SMILE TODAY:

_____

_____

_____

_____

_____

_____

DATE: ___/___/___

THIS SMILE WAS THE SOURCE OF MY JOY TODAY:

_____

_____

_____

_____

_____

_____

SOMETIMES YOUR
JOY IS THE SOURCE
OF YOUR SMILE,
BUT SOMETIMES
YOUR SMILE CAN
BE THE SOURCE OF
YOUR JOY.

Thich Nhat Hanh

DATE: ___/___/___

OUR FIVE SENSES ARE INCOMPLETE WITHOUT THE SIXTH—A SENSE OF HUMOR.

William Arthur Ward

What stimulated my sixth sense today:

_____

_____

_____

_____

_____

Impropriety is the soul of wit.

W. Somerset Maugham

A witty impropriety that made me smile today:

_____

_____

_____

_____

_____

At painful times, when composition is impossible and reading is not *enough*, grammars and dictionaries are excellent for *distraction*.

Elizabeth Barrett Browning

Pick up a dictionary, open to a random page, and note down something distracting that makes you smile:

_____

_____

_____

_____

WORDPLAY

Definitions from Ambrose Bierce's *Devil's Dictionary* (1906)

ADMIRATION: Our polite recognition of another's resemblance to ourselves.

ARMOR: The kind of clothing worn by a person whose tailor is a blacksmith.

BORE: A person who talks when you wish him to listen.

HANDKERCHIEF: A small square of silk or linen, used in various ignoble offices about the face and especially serviceable at funerals to conceal the lack of tears.

MAYONNAISE: One of the sauces which serve the French in place of a state religion.

SELFISH: Devoid of consideration for the selfishness of others.

Write a definition here that would make Ambrose Bierce smile:

_____

There can be no other occupation like gardening in which, if you were to creep up behind someone at their work, you would find them smiling.

Mirabel Osler

_____ makes me smile, and that's why I go on doing it.

I'VE NEVER MISSED A GIG YET. MUSIC MAKES PEOPLE HAPPY, AND THAT'S WHY I GO ON DOING IT—I LIKE TO SEE EVERYBODY SMILE.

Buddy Guy

_____ makes people happy, and that's why I go on doing it.

Smile. Have you ever noticed how easily puppies make human friends? Yet all they do is wag their tails and fall over.

Walter Anderson

DATE: ___ /___ /___

A HUMAN FRIEND I MADE TODAY WITH A SMILE:

_____

_____

_____

_____

_____

_____

DATE: ___ /___ /___

AN ANIMAL FRIEND I MADE TODAY WITH A SMILE:

_____

_____

_____

_____

_____

_____

SMILE, IT CONFUSES PEOPLE.

Scott Adams

How I interpreted a confusing smile today:

_____

_____

_____

_____

_____

DATE: ___ / ___ / ___

THERE IS A SMILE OF LOVE,
AND THERE IS A SMILE OF DECEIT,
AND THERE IS A SMILE OF SMILES
IN WHICH THESE TWO SMILES MEET.

William Blake

How I interpreted a smile of smiles today:

_____

_____

_____

_____

_____

Turn this pear into one of these: ghost, lightbulb, baby, pigeon, elf, or something else.

Turn this pair of scissors into one of these: mother and baby, fish, dancers, mustached face, chicken, or something else.

DATE: ___ / ___ / ___

Science has found that the basic human nature is compassionate. Our basic nature is to be social, appreciate the other's kindness, smile.

14th Dalai Lama

My first compassionate smile of the day:

_____

_____

_____

_____

_____

EVERY HUMAN MIND FEELS PLEASURE IN DOING GOOD TO ANOTHER.

Thomas Jefferson

Doing this good deed today made me smile:

_____

_____

_____

_____

_____

DATE: ___ / ___ / ___

I WAS PAID WITH A SMILE FOR THIS TODAY:

_____

_____

_____

_____

_____

_____

DATE: ___ / ___ / ___

I REWARDED _____ **WITH A SMILE FOR THIS TODAY:**

_____

_____

_____

_____

_____

_____

A smile is often the essential. One is paid with a smile. One is rewarded by a smile.

Antoine de Saint-Exupéry

After every storm the sun will smile;
for every problem there is a solution,
and the soul's indefeasible duty is to
be of good cheer.

William R. Alger, attrib.

After struggling with a stormy problem, I came up with this solution:

_____

_____

_____

_____

Yay!

My heart today smiles at its past night of tears like a wet tree glistening in the sun after the rain is over.

Rabindranath Tagore

Why I am able to smile at the source of last night's tears today:

_____

_____

_____

_____

_____

Nothing can beat the smell of dew and flowers and the odor that comes out of the earth when the sun goes down.

Ethel Waters, attrib.

A smell in nature that made me smile today:

_____

_____

_____

_____

_____

SMILE

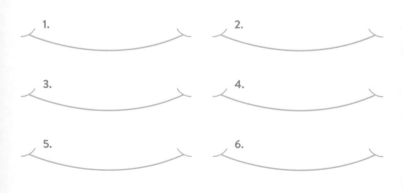

1.

2.

3.

4.

5.

6.

7.

8.

Waking up this morning, I smile. Twenty-four brand new hours are before me. I vow to live fully in each moment and to look at all beings with eyes of compassion.

Thich Nhat Hanh, attrib.

How greeting the morning with a smile set the pace for the rest of the day:

_____

_____

_____

_____

DATE: ___ / ___ / ___

IF YOU'RE NOT USING YOUR
SMILE, YOU'RE LIKE A MAN WITH
A MILLION DOLLARS IN THE BANK
AND NO CHECKBOOK.

Les Giblin, attrib.

How my smile paid off today:

_____

_____

_____

_____

_____

Mankind are always happy for having been happy, so that if you make them happy now, you make them happy twenty years hence by memory of it.

Sydney Smith

DATE: ___ / ___ / ___

HAPPY EVENT THAT MADE ME SMILE TODAY:

_____

_____

_____

_____

_____

_____

DATE: ___ / ___ / ___

MEMORY OF HAPPY EVENT _____ YEARS AGO THAT MADE ME SMILE TODAY:

_____

_____

_____

_____

_____

_____

Wear a smile and have friends, wear a scowl and have wrinkles.

F. O. Hamilton

New friends I attracted today with my smile:

_____

_____

_____

_____

_____

_____

WRINKLES SHOULD MERELY INDICATE WHERE SMILES HAVE BEEN.

Mark Twain

Draw your smile wrinkles:

DATE: ___ / ___ / ___

By Chivalries as tiny,
A Blossom or a Book,
The seeds of smiles are planted—
Which blossom in the dark.

Emily Dickinson

The seed of my smile today:

_____

_____

_____

_____

_____

DATE: ___ / ___ / ___

WHAT MADE ME SMILE TODAY · WHAT MADE ME SMILE TODAY

Complete one or more prompts:

Hearing a child say this: _____

A rainbow: _____

A thank you from: _____

The right gift to: _____

The right gift from: _____

Getting hooked on this book: _____

Good hair day: _____

Other: _____

DATE: ___/___/___

SMILE, FOR EVERYONE LACKS SELF-CONFIDENCE AND MORE THAN ANY OTHER ONE THING A SMILE REASSURES THEM.

André Maurois

_____'s smile reassured me today.

For ne'er
Was flattery lost on poet's ear:
A simple race! they waste their toil
For the vain tribute of a smile.

Sir Walter Scott

I earned a smile today for this creation:

_____

_____

_____

_____

_____

DATE: ___ / ___ / ___

SOMEONE WHO PERFECTLY SHARES MY IDEA OF BEING FUNNY:

_____

_____

_____

_____

_____

_____

DATE: ___ / ___ / ___

I'VE LEARNED OVER THE YEARS TO APPRECIATE _____ 'S
IDEA OF BEING FUNNY.

IT IS A DIFFICULT THING TO LIKE ANYBODY ELSE'S IDEAS OF BEING FUNNY.

Gertrude Stein

DATE: ___/___/___

THINKING A SMILE ALL THE TIME WILL KEEP YOUR FACE YOUTHFUL.

Gelett Burgess

How I used my beauty secret today:

_____

_____

_____

_____

_____

EVERY SMILE MAKES YOU A DAY YOUNGER.

Chinese proverb

How many days younger I am today, as of ____ : ____ P.M.:

_____

_____

_____

_____

_____

DATE: ___ / ___ / ___

When I make a mistake, it's a beaut!

Fiorello La Guardia

A beaut of a mistake that made me smile today:

_____

_____

_____

_____

_____

WORDPLAY

Misprints

Find the misprints and correct them. (See answers below.)

1. Thou shalt commit adultery. —*King James Bible* (1631 ed.)

2. Commencement 2012 Program for the Lyndon B. Johnson School of Pubic Affairs, University of Texas at Austin

3. . . . harmoniously abandoning themselves to the rhythm of the music— like two small chips being tossed about on a rough but friendly sea. —*An American Tragedy*, Theodore Dreiser

4. . . . a moment of panic before he saw him walking along the bench downshore. —*The Road*, Cormac McCarthy

5. He goosed the throttle and worked the wheel, using the four-wheeler's power rather than moist his strength to right the six-hundred-pound vehicle. —*Plague Ship*, Clive Cluster and Jack Du Brul

Answers: 1. not, 2. public, 3. ships, 4. beach, 5. hoist

IF YOU LAUGH WITH SOMEBODY, THEN YOU KNOW YOU SHARE SOMETHING.

Trevor Noah

Today _____ and I shared a laugh.

DATE: ___ / ___ / ___

Even if you cannot change all the people around you, you can change the people you choose to be around. . . . Spend your life with people who make you smile, laugh, and feel loved.

Roy T. Bennett

These are the people I chose to be around today:

_____

_____

_____

_____

_____

Be kind to yourself this evening. Buy something for yourself. Treat yourself to a meal. Look in the mirror and give yourself a smile.

Yoko Ono

DATE: ___/___/___

I BOUGHT THIS FOR MYSELF TODAY AND SMILED:

_____

_____

_____

_____

_____

_____

DATE: ___/___/___

I TREATED MYSELF TO THIS TODAY AND SMILED:

_____

_____

_____

_____

_____

MIRTH IS LIKE A FLASH OF LIGHTNING, THAT BREAKS THROUGH A GLOOM OF CLOUDS, AND GLITTERS FOR THE MOMENT.

Joseph Addison

A flash of mirth that broke through my gloom of clouds today:

_____

_____

_____

_____

_____

Humor is the great thing, the saving thing after all. The minute it crops up, all our hardnesses yield, all our irritations, and resentments flit away, and a sunny spirit takes their place.

Mark Twain

How humor saved me today:

_____

_____

_____

_____

_____

☐ I made a bunny move its ears with this hand shadow:

☐ I made a bird fly with this hand shadow:

DATE: ___/___/___

A smile is worth a thousand words.

American proverb

What _____'s smile said to me today:

_____

_____

_____

_____

_____

_____

Word count: _____

DATE: ___ / ___ / ___

A SMILE IS AS GOOD AS A PRAYER.

Abigail May Alcott Nieriker

This was my smiling prayer today:

_____

_____

_____

_____

_____

_____

It ☐ was   ☐ was not   answered.

DATE: ___/___/___

A SMILE AIMED AT JUST ME TODAY:

_____

_____

_____

_____

_____

_____

DATE: ___/___/___

A SMILE SHARED WITH OTHERS TODAY:

_____

_____

_____

_____

_____

_____

Oh, sir, she smiled
no doubt,
Whene'er I passed
her; but who
passed without
Much the same smile?

Robert Browning

We are not amused.

Queen Victoria

When I felt like quoting Queen Victoria today:

_____

_____

_____

_____

_____

DATE: ___/___/___

WHAT DO YOU MEAN, FUNNY? FUNNY PECULIAR OR FUNNY HA-HA?

Ian Hay

This was something ☐ funny peculiar ☐ funny ha-ha that made me smile today:

_____

_____

_____

_____

OUT WHERE THE HANDCLASP'S A LITTLE STRONGER,

OUT WHERE THE SMILE DWELLS A LITTLE LONGER,

THAT'S WHERE THE WEST BEGINS.

Arthur Chapman

A friendly spot that made me smile today:

_____

_____

_____

_____

_____

DATE: ___/___/___

PLACES

that always   make me

SMILE

1.

2.

3.

4.

5.

6.

7.

8.

THE MOST DIFFICULT PART IS TO GIVE, THEN WHY NOT ADD A SMILE?

Jean de La Bruyère

I added a smile to this gift today:

_____

_____

The response:

_____

_____

The man who gives little with a smile gives more than the man who gives much with a frown.

Jewish proverb

This is the little I gave today with a smile:

_____

_____

_____

_____

_____

Make two grins
grow where
there was only a
grouch before.

Elbert Hubbard

DATE: ___ / ___ / ___

HOW I MADE _____'S GROUCH INTO A GRIN TODAY:

_____

_____

_____

_____

_____

_____

DATE: ___ / ___ / ___

HOW _____ MADE MY GROUCH INTO A GRIN TODAY:

_____

_____

_____

_____

_____

_____

There was ease in Casey's manner as he stepped into his place,

There was pride in Casey's bearing, and a smile on Casey's face.

Ernest Lawrence Thayer

When there was ease in my manner, pride in my bearing, and a smile on my face today:

_____

_____

_____

_____

DATE: ___/___/___

I LIKE TO SEE THE SMILES ON PEOPLE'S FACES WHEN I SHOW THEM I CAN DO THE IMPOSSIBLE.

Marvin Hagler

An accomplishment today that made people smile:

_____

_____

_____

_____

_____

Someone says to me, "Jerry Lewis says women aren't funny," or "Christopher Hitchens says women aren't funny," or "Rick Fenderman says women aren't funny. . . . Do you have anything to say to that?" Yes. We don't [@#!!@!!] care if you like it. I don't say it out loud, of course, because Jerry Lewis is a great philanthropist, Hitchens is very sick, and the third guy I made up.

Tina Fey

My favorite women comedians:

_____

_____

_____

_____

_____

MVP moment [Most Valuable Player on a *30 Rock* episode]: Tracy Jordan admonishing a pigeon for eating out of the garbage. . . .

> **Stop eating people's old French fries, little pigeon. Have some self-respect. Don't you know you can fly?**

Overheard conversation with an animal that made me smile today:

_____

_____

_____

DATE: ___ / ___ / ___

I wanted to do another movie [*The Terminal*] that could make us laugh and cry and feel good about the world. . . . This is a time when we need to smile more and Hollywood movies are supposed to do that for people in difficult times.

Steven Spielberg

This movie made me laugh and feel good about the world:

_____

_____

_____

_____

_____

DATE: ___/___/___

YOU DANCE LOVE, AND YOU DANCE JOY, AND YOU
DANCE DREAMS. AND I KNOW IF I CAN MAKE YOU
SMILE BY JUMPING OVER A COUPLE OF COUCHES
OR RUNNING THROUGH A RAINSTORM, THEN I'LL BE
VERY GLAD TO BE A SONG AND DANCE MAN.

Gene Kelly

How I used my talent to make people smile today:

_____

_____

_____

_____

_____

DATE: ___/___/___

A MEMORY THAT VEILED MY SMILE AT _____ **TODAY:**

_____

_____

_____

_____

_____

_____

DATE: ___/___/___

A DREAM THAT TINGED MY SMILE AT _____ **TODAY:**

_____

_____

_____

_____

_____

_____

HE SMILED THE
MOST EXQUISITE
SMILE, VEILED BY
MEMORY, TINGED
BY DREAMS.

Virginia Woolf

I feel very happy to see the sun come up every day. I feel happy to be around . . . I like to take this day—any day—and go to town with it.

James Dickey

How I went to town on this happy day:

_____

_____

_____

_____

_____

DATE: ___ / ___ / ___

As happy a man as any in the world, for the whole world seems to smile upon me!

Samuel Pepys

The whole world seemed to smile upon me today because:

_____

_____

_____

_____

_____

DATE: ___ / ___ / ___

HUMOR IS THE FIRST OF THE GIFTS TO PERISH IN A FOREIGN TONGUE.

Virginia Woolf

The multilingual joke below is ☐ funny, so Virginia Woolf is not so smart after all. ☐ not funny—Right on, Virginia!

Where do cats go when they die?

purrrgatory (English)

purrrgatorio (Italian and Spanish)

purrrgatório (Portuguese)

purrrgatoriu (Romanian)

purrrgatoire (French)

WORDPLAY

Translations of Common English Words

Match the English word in the first column with what it is called in another language in the second column. (See answers below.)

1. echo
2. stapler
3. drums
4. computer
5. Santa Claus

a) paper vampire (Afrikaans)
b) electric brain (Chinese)
c) rock language (Icelandic)
d) Christmas Goat (Finnish)
e) hit stuff (German)

Answers: 1. c, 2. a, 3. e, 4. b, 5. d

I'VE ALWAYS THOUGHT THE PRETTIEST SMILES ARE THE ONES THAT SHOW THE MOST TEETH.

D. W. Wilson

My favorite feature in a smile:

_____

_____

_____

_____

_____

_____

_____

Jemima was not pretty, the flatness and shortness of her face made her almost plain; yet most people looked twice at her expressive countenance, at the eyes which flamed or melted at every trifle, at the rich color which came at every expressed emotion into her usually sallow face, at the faultless teeth which made her smile like a sunbeam.

Elizabeth Gaskell

Check off the essential elements of a pretty face:

☐ expressive countenance

☐ eyes that flame or melt

☐ rich color of emotion

☐ faultless teeth

☐ sunny smile

☐ _____

<small>other</small>

Actions speak louder than words, and a smile says, "I like you. You make me happy. I am glad to see you."

Dale Carnegie

DATE: ___/___/___

MY SMILE AT _____ TODAY SAID:

_____

_____

_____

_____

_____

_____

DATE: ___/___/___

_____ 'S SMILE AT ME TODAY SAID:

_____

_____

_____

_____

_____

_____

DATE: ___/___/___

TRUE HUMOR SPRINGS NOT MORE FROM THE HEAD THAN FROM THE HEART. IT IS NOT CONTEMPT; ITS ESSENCE IS LOVE. IT ISSUES NOT IN LAUGHTER, BUT IN STILL SMILES, WHICH LIE FAR DEEPER.

Thomas Carlyle

The kind of humor that always makes me smile: ☐ wit or wordplay

☐ slapstick   ☐ dark   ☐ self-deprecating   ☐ improvisation

☐ _____
                other

IN THIS FOOLISH WORLD THERE IS NOTHING MORE NUMEROUS

THAN DIFFERENT PEOPLE'S SENSES OF HUMOROUS.

Ogden Nash

In my world, these wise people get my sense of humor:

_____

_____

_____

_____

_____

A smile recures the wounding of a frown.

William Shakespeare

Trick I used to turn a frown into a smile today:

_____

_____

_____

_____

_____

DATE: ___/___/___

How can you make a grumpy person smile? (See solution below.)

Solution: Turn him upside down.

I'm getting so old my insurance company sends me ½ a calendar!

Rodney Dangerfield

Something funny about getting old:

_____

_____

_____

_____

_____

DATE: __/__/__

ALL I ASK IS THE CHANCE TO PROVE THAT MONEY CAN'T MAKE ME HAPPY.

Spike Milligan

Something funny about money:

_____

_____

_____

_____

_____

DATE: ___ / ___ / ___

SIGHTS FROM NATURE THAT MADE ME SMILE TODAY:

_____

_____

_____

_____

_____

_____

DATE: ___ / ___ / ___

SOUNDS FROM NATURE THAT MADE ME SMILE TODAY:

_____

_____

_____

_____

_____

_____

How fair doth Nature
Appear again!
How bright the sunbeams!
How smiles the plain!
The flow'rs are bursting
From ev'ry bough,
And thousand voices
Each bush yields now.
And joy and gladness
Fill ev'ry breast!

Johann Wolfgang von Goethe

You must not ever stop being whimsical.

Mary Oliver

Something whimsical I did today that made me smile:

_____

_____

_____

_____

_____

IT IS NEITHER WEALTH NOR SPLENDOR; BUT TRANQUILITY AND OCCUPATION WHICH GIVE YOU HAPPINESS.

Thomas Jefferson

Kind of ☐ tranquility ☐ occupation that made me smile today:

_____

_____

_____

_____

_____

A game that keeps a smile on the player's face is a wonderful thing. Nintendo's theme for 2006 [was] "Create new fun." Spread the fun of games to everyone.

Shigeru Miyamoto

I spread the fun of _____ to _____ today.

GAMES
that always make me
SMILE

1.

2.

3.

4.

5.

6.

7.

8.

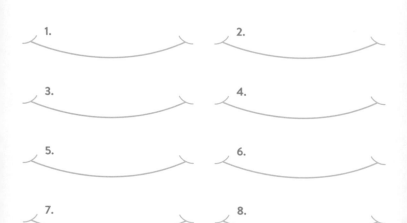

Laughter is regional: a smile extends over the whole face.

Malcolm de Chazal

Map the difference between laughter and a smile on these two faces:

DATE: ___ /___ /___

HE DOES SMILE HIS FACE INTO MORE LINES THAN IS IN THE NEW MAP WITH THE AUGMENTATION OF THE INDIES.

William Shakespeare

When I smile, I have _____ happy lines on my face.

A single
sunbeam is
enough to drive
away many
shadows.

St. Francis of Assisi

DATE: ___/___/___

A PERSONAL SUNBEAM THAT MADE ME SMILE TODAY:

_____

_____

_____

_____

_____

_____

DATE: ___/___/___

A WORK SUNBEAM THAT MADE ME SMILE TODAY:

_____

_____

_____

_____

_____

_____

She had not known before that it takes two to make a smile.

Laura Ingalls Wilder

My first smiling partner today:

_____

_____

The occasion:

_____

_____

DATE: ___ / ___ / ___

HER SMILE WAS NOT MEANT TO BE SEEN BY ANYONE AND SERVED ITS WHOLE PURPOSE IN BEING SMILED.

Rainer Maria Rilke

Purpose of my private smile today:

_____

_____

_____

_____

_____

The thing that goes the farthest toward making life worthwhile,

That costs the least, and does the most, is just a pleasant smile.

W. D. Nesbit

A pleasant smile was my winning lottery ticket today because:

_____

_____

_____

_____

_____

DATE: __ / __ / __

WHAT MADE ME SMILE TODAY · WHAT MADE ME SMILE TODAY

Complete one or more prompts:

Setting a new personal best: _____

Finishing this project: _____

This holiday tradition: _____

Seeing a baby do this: _____

My birthday today: _____

Listening to this: _____

This freebie: _____

Other: _____

DATE: ___ / ___ / ___

BEHOLD THE TURTLE. HE MAKES PROGRESS ONLY WHEN HE STICKS HIS NECK OUT.

James Bryant Conant

I took a chance with this ☐ friendly ☐ sympathetic ☐ flirtatious

☐ _____ smile today:
　　　　　other

_____

_____

_____

_____

Love makes even a turtle smile.

Henrietta Newton Martin

Love made even this turtle smile:

_____

_____

_____

_____

_____

DATE: ___ / ___ / ___

SPOTS I LIKE TO TICKLE:

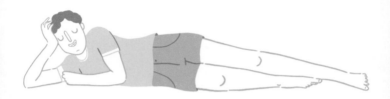

DATE: ___ / ___ / ___

SPOTS I LIKE TO BE TICKLED:

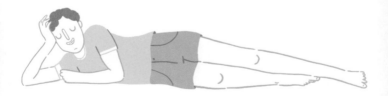

I THINK
EVERYONE IS
TICKLISH. YOU
JUST GOTTA FIND
THE RIGHT SPOTS.

Derek Jeter

DATE: ___ / ___ / ___

Of all life's blessings, none are cheaper or more easily dispensed than smiles. Let us not, then, be too chary of them, but scatter them freely as we go; for life is too short to be frowned away.

Massachusetts Society for the Prevention of Cruelty to Animals

Mark where you scattered smiles freely today.

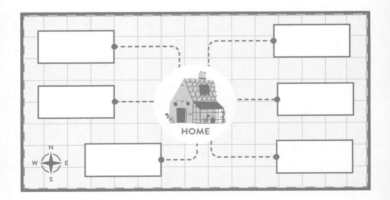

DATE: ___ / ___ / ___

You sell your smile for pennies! I tell you, it's not worth it. . . . Even if you are made the king or the emperor of the world, it's not worth giving away your smile.

Sri Sri Ravi Shankar

I saved my million-dollar smile for ☐ someone ☐ something

special today:

_____

_____

_____

_____

_____

_____

_____

DATE: ___/___/___

It is a sad truth,
but we have lost the
faculty of giving
lovely names to things.

Oscar Wilde

A lovely name I ☐ heard   ☐ read   ☐ made up   today:

_____

_____

_____

_____

_____

WORDPLAY

Technical Terms

Match the silly sounding but real words with their serious meanings. (See answers below.)

1. dysania
2. interrobang
3. minimus
4. overmorrow
5. vocables
6. wamble

a) rumbling of the stomach
b) day after tomorrow
c) combination of an exclamation point and a question mark
d) difficulty getting out of bed in the morning
e) baby toe or pinky finger
f) meaningless syllables in a song (e.g., la la la)

Answers: 1. d, 2. c, 3. e, 4. b, 5. f, 6. a

THY LOVING SMILE WILL SURELY HAIL THE LOVE-GIFT OF A FAIRYTALE.

Lewis Carroll

A love-gift that made me smile back today:

_____

_____

_____

_____

_____

DATE: __ / __ / __

FOCUS ON GIVING SMILES AWAY AND YOU WILL DISCOVER THAT YOUR OWN SMILES WILL ALWAYS BE IN GREAT SUPPLY!

Joyce Meyer

I gave these smiles away extravagantly today:

_____

_____

I ☐ do ☐ do not have one left to smile at myself in the mirror.

_____

_____

'Tis easy enough
to be pleasant,
When life flows along
like a song;
But the man worth
while is the one who
will smile
When everything goes
dead wrong.

Ella Wheeler Wilcox

DATE: ___/___/___

IT WAS EASY TO SMILE TODAY BECAUSE:

_____

_____

_____

_____

_____

_____

DATE: ___/___/___

IT WAS HARD TO SMILE TODAY BECAUSE:

_____

_____

_____

_____

_____

IN THE MODERN CONFLICT BETWEEN THE SMILE AND THE LAUGH, I AM ALL IN FAVOR OF LAUGHING.

G. K. Chesterton

Why laughs are better than smiles:

_____

_____

_____

_____

_____

I WAS LEARNING THAT AMONG FRIENDS, A SMILE CAN BE BETTER THAN A BELLY LAUGH.

Alan Bradley

Why smiles are better than laughs:

_____

_____

_____

_____

_____

Mark my words, when a society has to resort to the lavatory for its humor, the writing is on the wall.

Alan Bennett

Today I saw this written on _____ and smiled:

_____

_____

_____

_____

_____

Check the signs that make you smile.

"SMALL COFFEE"
$5

"SMALL COFFEE, PLEASE"
$3

"HELLO, ONE SMALL
COFFEE, PLEASE"
$1.75

☐

*A yawn
is a silent
scream
for coffee*

☐

IN WINE THERE IS WISDOM
IN BEER THERE IS STRENGTH
IN WATER THERE IS BACTERIA
YOU DECIDE

☐

EAT HERE
OR WE
BOTH
STARVE

☐

A genuine, affectionate smile is very important in our day-to-day lives.

14th Dalai Lama

List the most genuine, affectionate smiles you gave today and why:

_____

_____

_____

_____

_____

I REMEMBER THE NECKCURLS, LIMP AND DAMP AS TENDRILS,

AND HER QUICK LOOK, A SIDELONG PICKEREL SMILE.

Theodore Roethke

Draw a pickerel smile, shark smile, dolphin smile:

DATE: ___ /___ /___

I GAVE AN AMBIGUOUS SMILE TO _____ TODAY BECAUSE:

_____

_____

_____

_____

_____

_____

DATE: ___ /___ /___

HOW I INTERPRETED AN AMBIGUOUS SMILE FROM _____ TODAY:

_____

_____

_____

_____

_____

_____

A smile is the chosen vehicle for all ambiguities.

Herman Melville

When I saw it I knew I wanted to be smiled at like that.

Garth Greenwell

I searched out _____ today because I wanted to be smiled at like that.

DATE: ___/___/___

WHEN I FIRST SAW YOU
WITH YOUR SMILE SO TENDER,
MY HEART WAS CAPTURED,
MY SOUL SURRENDERED.

from Elvis Presley hit "It's Now or Never"
(by Aaron Schroeder and Wally Gold)

Smile that captured me, heart and soul, today:

_____

_____

_____

_____

_____

Among those whom I like or admire, I can find no common denominator, but among those whom I love, I can: all of them make me laugh.

W. H. Auden

People who made me laugh today:

_____

_____

_____

_____

_____

PEOPLE

who always   make me

SMILE

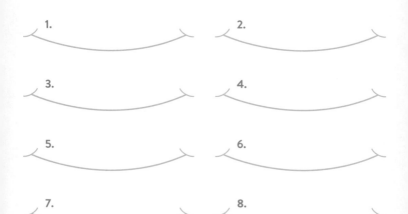

1.

2.

3.

4.

5.

6.

7.

8.

THE MONA LISA SMILES BECAUSE ALL THOSE WHO HAVE DRAWN A MUSTACHE ON HER ARE DEAD.

Unknown

Another explanation for Mona Lisa's smile. Not seriously:

_____

_____

_____

_____

_____

Mona Lisa must have had the highway blues; you can tell by the way she smiles.

Bob Dylan

What could be behind Mona Lisa's smile? Seriously:

_____

_____

_____

_____

_____

Hey, I've got nothing to do today but smile.

Paul Simon

DATE: ___/___/___

MY FIRST SMILE OF THE DAY WAS BECAUSE:

_____

_____

_____

_____

_____

_____

DATE: ___/___/___

MY LAST SMILE OF THE DAY WAS BECAUSE:

_____

_____

_____

_____

_____

Always keep your smile. That's how I explain my long life.

Jeanne Calment

Smiling helps you live a long life by (check one or more):

☐ reducing stress

☐ attracting friends

☐ confusing the enemy

☐ showing your teeth

☐ _____
other

THAT SMILE COULD END WARS AND CURE CANCER.

John Green

Example of a powerful smile today:

_____

_____

_____

_____

_____

_____

DATE: ___ / ___ / ___

You can tell a joke to your friends that you couldn't tell anywhere else because your friends know where you're coming from.

Trevor Noah

A joke I could tell only to my friends:

_____

_____

_____

_____

_____

> Is there one joke that always works? I don't think so. Maybe falling. Falling might be the only joke that works internationally. It's a joke where you are the punch line.

Slapstick gags that always make me smile:

- ☐ dramatic slips (on ice or a banana peel)
- ☐ umbrellas blown inside out
- ☐ fights with contactless punches
- ☐ food fights
- ☐ skidding chase scenes
- ☐ _____
  other

DATE: ___/___/___

IF I SMILE AT ANOTHER HUMAN BEING,
SHE OR HE GENERALLY SMILES IN RETURN,
AND EVEN ANIMALS SMILE IN RETURN.

14th Dalai Lama

Number of people who returned my smile today:

☐ 0   ☐ less than 5   ☐ more than 5

Number of animals that returned my smile today:

☐ 0   ☐ less than 5   ☐ more than 5

Your day will go the way the corners of your mouth turn.

Unknown

Set your face for the day.

How my day went:

_____

_____

DATE: ___/___/___

WHAT I DID TODAY THAT MADE ME SMILE WITH PRIDE:

_____

_____

_____

_____

_____

_____

DATE: ___/___/___

WHAT I DID TODAY THAT MADE ME SMILE WITH CONFIDENCE:

_____

_____

_____

_____

_____

_____

ORDINARILY, A PERSON
LEAVING A COURTROOM
WITH A CONVICTION
BEHIND HIM WOULD
WEAR A SOMBER FACE.
BUT I LEFT WITH A
SMILE. I KNEW THAT
I WAS A CONVICTED
CRIMINAL, BUT I WAS
PROUD OF MY CRIME.

Martin Luther King, Jr.

ART LINKLETTER: WHAT'S THE HARDEST THING ABOUT SCHOOL FOR YOU?

KID: BUTTONING MY PANTS.

Kids Say the Darndest Things (*TV show*)

Darndest thing I heard a kid say today:

_____

_____

_____

_____

_____

DATE: ___/___/___

The best wake-up call I know is to have my son smile at me in the morning.

Sean Pertwee

A wake-up call that made me smile this morning:

_____

_____

_____

_____

_____

The difference between the *almost right* word and the *right* word is really a large matter—'tis the difference between the lightning bug and the lightning.

Mark Twain

A malapropism that made me smile today:

_____

_____

_____

_____

_____

WORDPLAY

Malapropisms

Malapropisms are named for Mrs. Malaprop, a character in an eighteenth-century play who regularly mangles her words. Correct the errors in these sentences. (See answers below.)

1. He is the very pineapple of politeness. —MRS. MALAPROP

2. They said he had neurosis of the liver. —ARCHIE BUNKER

3. We need to look at the states, which are lavatories of innovation. —GOVERNOR RICK PERRY

4. Texas has a lot of electrical votes. —YOGI BERRA

5. What is all this talk about the Supreme Court decision on a deaf penalty? —GILDA RADNER

6. This makes me so sore it gets my dandruff up. —SAMUEL GOLDWYN

Answers: pinnacle, cirrhosis, laboratories, electoral, death, dander

DATE: ___ / ___ / ___

When she smiles, it feels like the first warm day of March—after an eternity of snow, when you suddenly remember how summer feels on the backs of your bare calves and in the part of your hair.

Jodi Picoult

When _____ smiles, it feels like the first warm day of March.

A SMILE IS THE SAME AS SUNSHINE; IT BANISHES WINTER FROM THE HUMAN COUNTENANCE.

Victor Hugo

Another reason why a smile is the same as sunshine:

_____

_____

_____

_____

_____

If you have made another person on this earth smile, your life has been worthwhile.

Sr. Mary Christelle Macaluso

DATE: ___/___/___

I MADE _____ SMILE TODAY BY:

_____

_____

_____

_____

_____

_____

DATE: ___/___/___

_____ MADE ME SMILE TODAY BY:

_____

_____

_____

_____

_____

_____

The most beautiful smile is the one for someone who isn't there, who just popped into your mind.

Ahlam Mosteghanemi

_____ popped into my mind and made me smile today.

WHEN LIFE TAKES ME ON A NEW JOURNEY, I SIMPLY REMEMBER THE SMILE MY FIRST BALLET RECITAL PUT ON MY FACE AND I MOVE FORWARD.

Andrea Thompson

A remembered smile that gives me courage:

_____

_____

_____

_____

_____

Describe what problem this image, by W. Heath Robinson, is solving.
(See answer below.)

_____

_____

_____

_____

_____

Answer: How to get to bed after a late night without disturbing the household

DATE: ___/___/___

Describe what problem this image, by W. Heath Robinson, is solving.
(See answer below.)

_____

_____

_____

_____

_____

You can tell how smart people are by what they laugh at.

Tina Fey

These geniuses always laugh at my jokes:

_____

_____

_____

_____

_____

THE HAPPY SAY YES. THE SUCCESSFUL SAY NO. THE PEACEFUL DO THEIR DUTY. THE WISE SMILE.

Maxime Lagacé

Why I was wise to smile today:

_____

_____

_____

_____

_____

DATE: ___/___/___

DESCRIBE THE BIGGEST SMILE YOU SAW TODAY:

_____

_____

_____

_____

_____

_____

DATE: ___/___/___

DRAW THE BIGGEST SMILE YOU SAW TODAY:

His smile was so wide he'd have had to break it into sections to fit it through a doorway.

Jerry Spinelli

DATE: ___/___/___

BE THE REASON SOMEONE SMILES. BE THE REASON SOMEONE FEELS LOVED AND BELIEVES IN THE GOODNESS IN PEOPLE.

Roy T. Bennett

I ☐ said ☐ did something that made _____ smile today:

_____

_____

_____

_____

_____

Improving our world one smile at a time.

World Smile Foundation

One small way I've improved the world:

_____

_____

_____

_____

_____

IF YOU'RE GOING TO AMERICA, BRING YOUR OWN FOOD.

Fran Lebowitz

Mark the countries on this map whose cuisines make you smile:

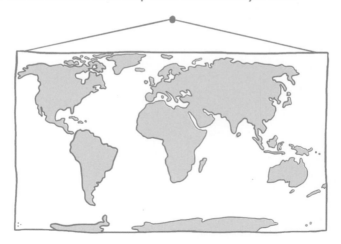

DATE: __/__/__

FOODS
that always *make me*
SMILE

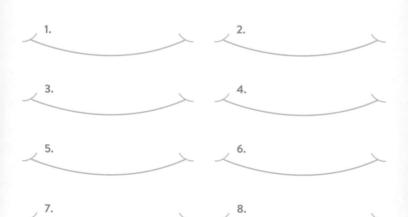

1.

2.

3.

4.

5.

6.

7.

8.

And the smile that is worth the praises of earth,

Is the smile that shines through tears.

Ella Wheeler Wilcox

Today my smile deserved the praises of earth because:

_____

_____

_____

_____

_____

A man with mirth is like a chariot with springs, in which one can ride over the roughest road, and scarcely feel anything but a pleasant rocking motion.

Henry Ward Beecher

Today I was able to ride with mirth over the roughest road because:

_____

_____

_____

_____

_____

They might not need
me—yet they might.
I'll let my Heart be
just in sight—
A smile so small as
mine might be
Precisely their necessity.

Emily Dickinson

DATE: ___ / ___ / ___

I GAVE A FRIEND MY SMALL SMILE TODAY BECAUSE:

_____

_____

_____

_____

_____

_____

DATE: ___ / ___ / ___

I GAVE A STRANGER MY SMALL SMILE TODAY BECAUSE:

_____

_____

_____

_____

_____

DATE: __ / __ / __

If you smile when no one else is around, you really mean it.

Andy Rooney

Why I smiled when no one else was around today:

_____

_____

_____

_____

_____

There can never be enough said of the virtues, the dangers, the powers of a shared laugh.

Françoise Sagan

The ☐ virtue ☐ danger ☐ power of the laugh I shared with

_____ today:

_____

_____

_____

_____

DATE: ___/___/___

The happiness of life is made up of minute fractions—the little, soon forgotten charities of a kiss or a smile, a kind look, a heartfelt compliment.

Samuel Taylor Coleridge

A minute fraction of life that made me smile today:

_____

_____

_____

_____

_____

WHAT MADE ME SMILE TODAY · WHAT MADE ME SMILE TOD

Complete one or more prompts:

Personal compliment: _____

Professional compliment: _____

This scent: _____

A run outdoors: _____

Thinking about this: _____

Winning this: _____

Watching my team win this: _____

Other: _____

FILM TITLE	TRANSLATION
The Full Monty	*Six Naked Pigs* (China)
Die Hard with a Vengeance	*Mega Hard* (Denmark)
The Naked Gun	*The Gun Died Laughing* (Israel)
Grease	*Vaseline* (Argentina)
Home Alone	*Mom, I Missed the Plane* (France)
The Parent Trap	*A Twin Seldom Comes Home Alone* (Germany)
Annie Hall	*Urban Neurotic* (Germany)

Translated film titles that made me smile:

_____

_____

Translated film titles that made me laugh:

_____

_____

COMEDY, WE MAY SAY, IS SOCIETY PROTECTING ITSELF— WITH A SMILE.

J. B. Priestley

A comedy that helped me to escape today:

_____

_____

_____

_____

_____

DATE: ___ /___ /___

SOMETHING I LAUGHED AT WHEN I WAS ALONE TODAY:

_____

_____

_____

_____

_____

_____

DATE: ___ /___ /___

SOMETHING I LAUGHED AT WHEN I WAS WITH OTHERS TODAY:

_____

_____

_____

_____

_____

_____

A LAUGH IS A SMILE THAT BURSTS.

Mary H. Waldrip

A SMILE IS THE UNIVERSAL WELCOME.

Max Eastman

Someone I welcomed today with a smile:

_____

_____

_____

_____

_____

DATE: ___ / ___ / ___

IF YOU'VE EVER BEEN HOMESICK OR FELT EXILED FROM ALL THE THINGS AND PEOPLE THAT ONCE DEFINED YOU, YOU'LL KNOW HOW IMPORTANT WELCOMING WORDS AND FRIENDLY SMILES CAN BE.

Stephen King

A friendly welcome today that made me smile:

_____

_____

_____

_____

_____

The name we give to something shapes our attitude toward it.

Katherine Paterson

A place I always smile at because of its name:

_____

_____

_____

_____

_____

WORDPLAY

Place Names

Choose the name of the real town in each state. (See answers below.)

ARIZONA: How *or* Why

ILLINOIS: Oblong *or* Square

KENTUCKY: Barefoot *or* Naked

NEW YORK: Commode *or* Flushing

OREGON: Zigzag *or* Spiral

TEXAS: Smile *or* Wink

Answers: Why, Oblong, Barefoot, Flushing, Zigzag, Wink

DATE: ___ / ___ / ___

[S]miling himself by anticipation, it was his fate to draw from the lady a more exquisite smile than the last. Smile the second made his heart beat so he could feel it against his waistcoat.

Charles Reade

Describe a smiling exchange you had today:

_____

_____

_____

_____

_____

DATE: ___/___/___

They gave each other a smile with a future in it.

Ring Lardner

Today I think _____ gave me a smile with a future in it.

Is a smile a question? Or is it the answer?

Lee Smith

DATE: ___/___/___

A QUESTION I ASKED WITH A SMILE TODAY:

_____

_____

_____

_____

_____

_____

DATE: ___/___/___

AN ANSWER I GAVE WITH A SMILE TODAY:

_____

_____

_____

_____

_____

_____

No matter how grouchy you're feeling,
You'll find the smile more or less healing.
It grows in a wreath
All around the front teeth—
Thus preserving the face from congealing.

Anthony Euwer

Draw a congealed grouchy face. In another color, heal it with a smile.

START EVERY DAY OFF WITH A SMILE AND GET IT OVER WITH.

W. C. Fields

Most endearing grouch in my family:

_____

_____

_____

_____

_____

_____

_____

DATE: ___/___/___

DO YOU THINK THAT WHEN THEY ASKED GEORGE WASHINGTON FOR ID THAT HE JUST WHIPPED OUT A QUARTER?

Steven Wright

Draw a picture of yourself smiling on this ID:

IDENTIFICATION CARD	
	Name
	_____
	_____

Make George Washington Smile

Make three folds in a dollar bill: in the middle of one eye, in the middle of the other eye, and another fold between these two. Crease well. Then take the bill in both your hands and wave it in front of you.

☐ I made George smile.

A smile is a powerful weapon; you can even break ice with it.

Unknown

The funniest icebreaker:

_____

_____

_____

_____

_____

BEAUTY IS POWER: A SMILE IS ITS SWORD.

Charles Reade

How I slayed with my beautiful smile today:

_____

_____

_____

_____

_____

DATE: ___ / ___ / ___

A WAG WHO MADE ME SMILE TODAY:

_____

_____

_____

_____

_____

_____

DATE: ___ / ___ / ___

MY SUCCESSFUL ATTEMPT TO BE A WAG TODAY (I SMILED TOO):

_____

_____

_____

_____

_____

_____

Every man has, some time in his life, an ambition to be a wag.*

Samuel Johnson

◆

*WAG. n.s. [wægan, Saxon, to cheat.] Anyone ludicrously mischievous;
a merry droll.
From *A Dictionary of the English Language* (1755), Samuel Johnson

DATE: ___/___/___

THE WISEST AMONG US—THE GENUINE LEADERS—SMILE IN THE FACE OF ADVERSITY.

Robin Sharma

Leader, boss, coach or _____ who made hard work more fun today:

_____

_____

_____

_____

_____

_____

_____

What's the use of worrying?
It never was worthwhile, so
Pack up your troubles in your old kit-bag
And smile, smile, smile.

George Asaf

Pack this bag with your troubles—and smile.

DATE: ___ /___ /___

MY HEART LEAPS UP WHEN I BEHOLD A RAINBOW IN THE SKY.

William Wordsworth

A sight outdoors that made me smile today:

_____

_____

_____

_____

_____

SIGHTS
that always make me
SMILE

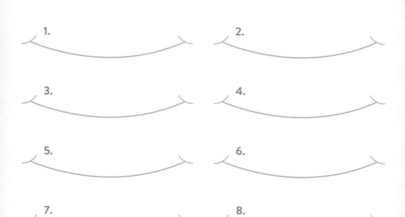

1.

2.

3.

4.

5.

6.

7.

8.

DATE: ___ /___ /___

From the time you were very little, you've had people who have smiled you into smiling, people who have talked you into talking, sung you into singing, loved you into loving.

Fred Rogers

These people smiled me into smiling today:

_____

_____

_____

_____

CHILDREN LEARN TO SMILE FROM THEIR PARENTS.

Shinichi Suzuki

What my parents taught me about smiling:

_____

_____

_____

_____

_____

How easy it is for one benevolent being to diffuse pleasure around him; and how truly is a kind heart a fountain of gladness, making everything in its vicinity to freshen into smiles! The joyous disposition of the worthy squire was perfectly contagious . . . and the little eccentricities of his humor did but season, in a manner, the sweetness of his philanthropy.

Washington Irving

DATE: ___ / ___ / ___

A GATHERING THAT BROUGHT A SMILE TO MY FACE TODAY:

_____

_____

_____

_____

_____

_____

DATE: ___ / ___ / ___

HUMOR THAT SEASONED A JOYOUS GATHERING TODAY:

_____

_____

_____

_____

_____

_____

DATE: ___/___/___

Most smiles are started by another smile.

Frank Howard Clark

_____ smiled and lit my first smile of the day.

Remember that happiness is as contagious as gloom. It should be the first duty of those who are happy to let others know of their gladness.

Maurice Maeterlinck, attrib.

Happiness I shared today:

_____

_____

_____

_____

_____

IN COMEDY . . . I'VE COME TO UNDERSTAND THAT JUST SMILING AND THE SPREAD OF GOODWILL MIGHT BE A HIGHER ART FORM THAN REALLY HEAVY, HARD LAUGHTER. WHENEVER I THINK OF CHAPLIN, I SMILE MORE THAN I LAUGH OUT LOUD.

Norm Macdonald

Comedians who make me smile:

_____

_____

_____

_____

_____

DATE: ___/___/___

COMICS' FAVORITE JOKES

NORM MACDONALD

This was Macdonald's "favorite stand-up joke ever," which he heard David Letterman tell:

> I was on the street the other day and I saw a garbage truck, and on the back of the garbage truck there was a small sign that said, 'Please do not follow too closely.' Another of life's simple pleasures ruined by meddling bureaucracy, ladies and gentlemen. Remember the old days when Dad would pile the kids in the station wagon and we'd all go out and follow a garbage truck?

An oldie-but-goodie that still makes me smile:

_____

_____

_____

To meditate, only you must smile. Smile with face, smile with mind, and good energy will come to you and clean away dirty energy. Even smile in your liver.

Elizabeth Gilbert

Pick a meditation exercise that works for you. Smile with your whole body while you are doing it, not just with your mouth. How did it feel?

_____

_____

_____

_____

BREATHING IN, I CALM MY BODY. BREATHING OUT, I SMILE.

Thich Nhat Hanh

Do this breathing exercise for two minutes: Calm on the in-breath, smile on the out-breath. How did it feel?

_____

_____

_____

_____

DATE: ___/___/___

RELATIVE WHO LOOKS NICER WITH A SMILE:

_____

_____

_____

_____

_____

_____

DATE: ___/___/___

FRIEND WHO LOOKS NICER WITH A SMILE:

_____

_____

_____

_____

_____

_____

IT MADE HER
THINK THAT IT
WAS CURIOUS
HOW MUCH
NICER A PERSON
LOOKED WHEN
HE SMILED.

Frances Hodgson Burnett

Be thou the rainbow to the storms of life,

The evening beam that smiles the clouds away,

And tints tomorrow with prophetic ray.

Lord Byron

The rainbow that chased my troubles away today:

_____

_____

_____

_____

_____

_____

DATE: ___ / ___ / ___

How true it is that, if we are cheerful and contented, all nature smiles, the air seems more balmy, the sky clearer, the earth has a brighter green . . . the flowers are more fragrant . . . and the sun, moon, and stars all appear more beautiful, and seem to rejoice with us.

Orison Swett Marden

Draw something in nature that made you smile today:

HONEST CRITICISM IS HARD TO TAKE, PARTICULARLY FROM A RELATIVE, A FRIEND, AN ACQUAINTANCE OR A STRANGER.

Franklin P. Jones

Honest praise always makes me smile. Praise I received today from a

☐ relative ☐ friend ☐ competitor ☐ acquaintance ☐ stranger:

_____

_____

_____

_____

DATE: ___/___/___

WORDPLAY

Bad Reviews

Check the bad reviews that make you smile:

☐ Wagner's music is better than it sounds. —EDGAR WILSON NYE

☐ Her only flair is in her nostrils. —PAULINE KAEL

☐ The covers of this book are too far apart. —AMBROSE BIERCE

☐ The play was a great success, but the audience was a disaster.
   —GEORGE BERNARD SHAW

☐ Your manuscript is both good and original, but the part that is good is
   not original and the part that is original is not good.
   —SAMUEL JOHNSON

☐ I would rather eat a golf ball than see this movie again.
   —ROGER EBERT

SMILE, IT'S FREE THERAPY.

Douglas Horton

How a smile lifted my mood today:

_____

_____

_____

_____

_____

_____

A smile is a face-lift that's in everyone's price range.

Tom Wilson

My smile makes my face look:

- ☐ more youthful
- ☐ brighter
- ☐ rosier
- ☐ happier
- ☐ _____
  other

Oh, you'll not be any poorer
if you smile along your way,
And your lot will not be harder
for the kindly things you say.
Don't imagine you are wasting
time for others that you spend:
You can rise to wealth and glory
and still pause to be a friend.

Edgar A. Guest

DATE: __/__/__

I SMILED ALONG MY WAY TO _____ TODAY. HOW PASSERSBY
RESPONDED:

_____

_____

_____

_____

_____

DATE: __/__/__

I RECEIVED _____ SMILES ALONG MY WAY TO _____
TODAY. HOW THEY MADE ME FEEL:

_____

_____

_____

_____

_____

DATE: ___ / ___ / ___

SMILE, DAMN IT!! SMILE.

Dame Sibyl Hathaway

Today I was ordered to smile for the camera. Attach photo here:

DATE: ___/___/___

PEOPLE WHO KEEP STIFF UPPER LIPS FIND THAT IT'S DAMN HARD TO SMILE.

Judith Guest

Look in the mirror and try to smile with a stiff upper lip.

I look ☐ happy   ☐ sad   ☐ ridiculous.

Illustrate these words or expressions with your own rebuses.

Forehead	Broken Heart
Tea Bag	Up to You
Many Thanks	Honey Bee

Solve these rebus puzzles by writing the words or expressions they illustrate. (See answers below.)

Get it Get it Get it Get it	Try $\dfrac{\text{stand}}{2}$
$\dfrac{\text{TRAVEL}}{\text{ccccccc}}$	**FAST**
EYE EYE	father

DATE: ___/___/___

WHEN YOU DO LAUGH, OPEN YOUR MOUTH WIDE
ENOUGH FOR THE NOISE TO GET OUT WITHOUT
SQUEALING, THROW YOUR HEAD BACK AS THOUGH
YOU WERE GOING TO BE SHAVED, HOLD ON TO YOUR
FALSE HAIR WITH BOTH HANDS, AND THEN LAUGH TILL
YOUR SOUL GETS THOROUGHLY RESTED.

Josh Billings

Describe how you produce a smile in 4 steps:

1. _____

2. _____

3. _____

4. _____

If you have only one smile in you, give it to the people you love. Don't be surly at home, then go out in the street and start grinning "Good morning" at total strangers.

Maya Angelou

Smiles today for the people I love:

_____

_____

_____

_____

_____

_____

DATE: ___/___/___

SILLY THING I DID ALONE TODAY TO MAKE MYSELF SMILE:

_____

_____

_____

_____

_____

_____

DATE: ___/___/___

SILLY THING I DID WITH OTHERS TODAY THAT MADE ME SMILE:

_____

_____

_____

_____

_____

I have always seen comedy as a lifeline. . . . When the pandemic was at full force, I grabbed my family and made a really silly movie. . . . It gave me purpose: to be ridiculous. . . . It also got me out of the house and into a community of people with the same goal—to make people smile.

Judd Apatow

Then a strange thing happened. She turned to him and smiled, and as he saw her smile every rag of anger and hurt vanity dropped from him.

F. Scott Fitzgerald

How I was cheered by a smile today:

_____

_____

_____

_____

_____

A SMILE CONFUSES AN APPROACHING FROWN.

Unknown

I smiled directly at someone who was frowning today. The response:

_____

_____

_____

_____

_____

Rate these silly song titles by adding 1 to 5 smiles.

"I Love You, You're
Perfect, Now Change"
JOE DIPIETRO

"Flushed from the
Bathroom of Your Heart"
JOHNNY CASH

"If the Phone Doesn't
Ring, It's Me"
JIMMY BUFFETT

"Put Your Big Toe in the
Milk of Human Kindness"
ELVIS COSTELLO

"Itsy Bitsy Teenie Weenie
Yellow Polka Dot Bikini"
BRIAN HYLAND

DATE: ___/___/___

MUSIC
that always   makes me
SMILE

1.

2.

3.

4.

5.

6.

7.

8.

AND THERE WAS SOMETHING SO ARTLESS IN THIS SMILE THAT I HAD TO SMILE BACK.

James Baldwin

I couldn't resist smiling back at _____ today.

DATE: ___ / ___ / ___

The world is a looking glass and gives back to every man the reflection of his own face.

Frown at it and it will in turn look sourly upon you; laugh at it and with it, and it is a jolly, kind companion.

William Makepeace Thackeray

Today I went to the mirror to join a jolly, kind companion.

I did it ☐ with a laugh   ☐ with a smile

It's hard to be funny when you have to be clean.

Mae West

DATE: ___ /___ /___

AN R-RATED JOKE THAT MADE ME SMILE TODAY:

_____

_____

_____

_____

_____

_____

DATE: ___ /___ /___

A PG-RATED JOKE THAT MADE ME SMILE TODAY:

_____

_____

_____

_____

_____

_____

You're never fully dressed without a smile.

Martin Charnin

Finish dressing these people:

A smile is the best makeup any girl can wear.

Marilyn Monroe

Self-portrait of me wearing my "makeup":

REMEMBER THIS— THAT VERY LITTLE IS NEEDED TO MAKE A HAPPY LIFE.

Marcus Aurelius

Something very little that brought me a big smile today:

_____

_____

_____

_____

_____

DATE: __/__/__

WHAT MADE ME SMILE TODAY · WHAT MADE ME SMILE TODAY

Complete one or more prompts:

Looking forward to: _____

Remembering: _____

Seeing an animal do this: _____

Hanging out with: _____

A friend's success: _____

Fresh sheets: _____

Tasting this: _____

Other: _____

DATE: ___ /___ /___

Certain images tattoo themselves on our brains and remain there without our permission, haunting us with nightmares or tickling us with delight.

Kathleen Parker

Draw a delightful image tattooed in your mind:

IT'S A GOOD DEED TO FORGET A POOR JOKE.

Brendan Bracken

I forgot the poor joke _____ told today.

(I do remember all the groaning.)

DATE: ___/___/___

INTENT OF MY SWEET SMILE AND SOFT WORD TODAY:

_____

_____

_____

_____

_____

_____

DATE: ___/___/___

EFFECT OF MY SWEET SMILE AND SOFT WORD TODAY:

_____

_____

_____

_____

_____

_____

A SWEET SMILE AND A SOFT WORD HAVE USUALLY THEIR DESIRED EFFECT.

Letitia Elizabeth Landon

DATE: ___/___/___

Anyone who takes himself too seriously always runs the risk of looking ridiculous; anyone who can consistently laugh at himself does not.

Václav Havel

Why I laughed at myself today:

_____

_____

_____

_____

_____

For what do we live, but to make sport for our neighbors, and laugh at them in our turn?

Jane Austen

How ☐ I made sport for my neighbors   ☐ my neighbors made sport for me today:

_____

_____

_____

_____

BROADLY SPEAKING, SHORT WORDS ARE BEST, AND THE OLD WORDS, WHEN SHORT, ARE BEST OF ALL.

Winston Churchill

A short word that made me smile today:

_____

WORDPLAY

Neologisms

Match the invented words from *Washington Post* contests with their definition. (See answers below.)

1. bozone
2. ignoranus
3. intaxication
4. karmageddon
5. laissez-fairy
6. sarchasm

a) euphoria at getting a tax refund

b) when everyone is sending off negative vibes

c) gulf between the person who makes a sarcastic remark and someone who doesn't get it

d) someone who thinks the market should determine the fair price for a lost tooth

e) substance surrounding stupid people that stops bright ideas from penetrating

f) a person who's both stupid and a butthead

Answers: 1. e, 2. f, 3. a, 4. b, 5. d, 6. c

DATE: ___/___/___

I LOVE THE MAN THAT CAN SMILE IN TROUBLE, THAT CAN GATHER STRENGTH FROM DISTRESS, AND GROW BRAVE BY REFLECTION.

Thomas Paine

I smiled down this trouble today:

_____

_____

_____

_____

_____

I think luck is the sense to recognize an opportunity and the ability to take advantage of it . . . The man who can smile at his breaks and grab his chances gets on.

Samuel Goldwyn

A lucky break I smiled at today:

_____

_____

_____

_____

_____

Count your life by smiles, not tears.

Dixie Willson

DATE: ___ / ___ / ___

LIST SOME SMILES TO DATE:

_____

_____

_____

_____

_____

_____

DATE: ___ / ___ / ___

LIST SOME SMILES TO DATE:

_____

_____

_____

_____

_____

_____

How does love speak?
In the faint flush upon the telltale cheek,
And in the pallor that succeeds it; by
The quivering of an averted eye—
The smile that proves the parent to a sigh
Thus doth love speak.

Ella Wheeler Wilcox

How someone spoke to me in the language of love today:

☐ flushed cheek ☐ averted eye

☐ smile and sigh ☐ _____
                              other

_____

_____

_____

DATE: __/__/__

Smiles are the language of love.

David Hare, attrib.

Words that made me smile and feel loved today:

_____

_____

_____

_____

_____

A pat on the back is only a few vertebrae removed from a kick in the pants, but is miles ahead in results.

Ella Wheeler Wilcox, attrib.

A pat on the back I received today from _____ for _____ :

_____

_____

_____

_____

_____

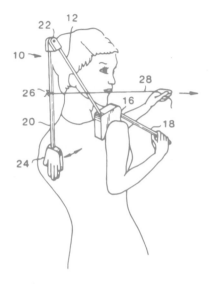

What is silly about this invention for patting yourself on the back?

_____

_____

_____

_____

_____

DATE: ___ / ___ / ___

I BELIEVE WE SHOULD ALL PAY OUR TAX BILL WITH A SMILE, BUT WHEN I TRIED, THEY WANTED CASH.

Unknown

An expression, punchline, cartoon caption, or other one-liner that made me smile today:

_____

_____

_____

_____

DATE: ___ / ___ / ___

"WHAT HO!" I SAID.

"WHAT HO!" SAID MOTTY.

"WHAT HO! WHAT HO!"

"WHAT HO! WHAT HO! WHAT HO!"

AFTER THAT IT SEEMED RATHER DIFFICULT TO GO ON WITH THE CONVERSATION.

P. G. Wodehouse

A ridiculous conversation I overheard and smiled at today:

_____

_____

_____

_____

_____

DATE: ___/___/___

A HAPPY THING THAT MADE ME SMILE TODAY:

_____

_____

_____

_____

_____

_____

DATE: ___/___/___

A HAPPY THING THAT MADE ME CRY TODAY (FOR EXAMPLE, A WEDDING):

_____

_____

_____

_____

_____

_____

Smiles and tears are so alike with me, they are neither of them confined to any particular feelings: I often cry when I am happy, and smile when I am sad.

Anne Brontë

Strange children should smile at each other and say, "Let's play."

F. Scott Fitzgerald

Today I smiled at someone new and said:

_____

_____

_____

_____

_____

DATE: ___/___/___

YOUTH SMILES WITHOUT ANY REASON. IT IS ONE OF ITS CHIEFEST CHARMS.

Oscar Wilde

I smiled without any reason today. My age: _____

THE FIRST TIME I SEE A JOGGER SMILING, I'LL CONSIDER IT.

Joan Rivers

New sports I would consider because I've seen players smiling:

_____

_____

_____

DATE: ___/___/___

SPORTS
that always make me
SMILE

1.

2.

3.

4.

5.

6.

7.

8.

Today, give a stranger one of your smiles. It might be the only sunshine he sees all day.

H. Jackson Brown, Jr.

I gave a stranger a smile today. The reaction:

_____

_____

_____

_____

_____

DATE: ___ / ___ / ___

NEVER A LIP IS CURVED WITH PAIN

THAT CAN'T BE KISSED INTO SMILES AGAIN.

Bret Harte

Today I was kissed by _____.

Oh joy, oh rapture!

It was a lovely day of blue skies and gentle breezes. Bees buzzed, birds tootled, and squirrels bustled to and fro getting their suntan in the bright sunshine. In a word, all Nature smiled.

P. G. Wodehouse

DATE: ___ / ___ / ___

DESCRIBE HOW NATURE SMILED TODAY:

_____

_____

_____

_____

_____

_____

DATE: ___ / ___ / ___

DRAW HOW NATURE SMILED TODAY:

A DAY WITHOUT SUNSHINE IS LIKE, YOU KNOW, NIGHT.

Steve Martin

A day without a smile is like, you know, _____ .

It was only a sunny smile, and little it cost in the giving, but like morning light it scattered the night and made the day worth living.

F. Scott Fitzgerald

A smile that made today worth living:

_____

_____

_____

_____

_____

If you're not easily irritated, I think it's hard to be funny.

Jerry Seinfeld

How I turned an irritation into something funny today and changed my

crankiness into a smile:

_____

_____

_____

_____

> Whenever my kids ask me [my favorite joke],
> I always answer with: 'Two peanuts were walking
> along; one was assaulted.'. . . I like that joke
> because anybody can tell it, and it always works.
> And it's very short.

My no-fail joke:

_____

_____

_____

All the awards in the world . . . [but there is] nothing better than walking into your dad's restaurant and seeing a smile on his face and knowing that your mom and dad and your sister are real proud of you.

Lady Gaga

People whose smiles are better than all the awards in the world:

_____

_____

_____

_____

_____

My mom smiled at me. Her smile kind of hugged me.

R. J. Palacio

My _____'s smile hugged me today.

DATE: ___/___/___

I DECIDED TO GIVE UP _____ TODAY

BECAUSE IT DOESN'T MAKE ME SMILE.

DATE: ___/___/___

I DECIDED TO DO MORE _____ TODAY

BECAUSE IT ALWAYS MAKES ME SMILE.

THERE IS NO
POINT TO
SAMBA IF IT
DOESN'T MAKE
YOU SMILE.

Alma Guillermoprieto

WE DON'T LAUGH BECAUSE WE'RE HAPPY, WE ARE HAPPY BECAUSE WE LAUGH.

William James

Laughing with _____ made me feel happy today.

Let your smile change the world! Never let the world change your smile!

Sri Sri Ravi Shankar

How my smile helped change the world for someone today:

_____

_____

_____

_____

_____

Proverbs put old heads on young shoulders.

Charles Reader

Channel your wisdom into a proverb that brings a smile to your face:

_____

_____

_____

_____

_____

WORDPLAY

Proverbs

Check the proverbs that make you smile:

☐ To lengthen your life, shorten your meals.

☐ A lover mistakes a pimple for a dimple.

☐ Tomorrow is often the busiest day of the year.

☐ If you pay peanuts, you get monkeys.

☐ Absence makes the heart go wander.

DATE: ___ /___ /___

HUMOR IS BY FAR THE MOST SIGNIFICANT ACTIVITY OF THE HUMAN BRAIN.

Edward de Bono

My most significant activity today:

_____

_____

_____

_____

_____

To succeed in life, you need three things: a wishbone, a backbone, and a funny bone.

Reba McEntire

How my funny bone helped me succeed today:

_____

_____

_____

_____

_____

Let us always meet each other with a smile, for the smile is the beginning of love.

Mother Teresa

DATE: ___/___/___

TODAY I SHOWED MY LOVE FOR _____ **WITH A SMILE.**

DATE: ___/___/___

TODAY _____ **'S SMILE MADE ME FEEL LOVED.**

DATE: __/__/__

I MUST GO INTO EXILE. DOES ANY MAN HINDER ME FROM GOING WITH SMILES AND CHEERFULNESS AND CONTENTMENT?

Epictetus

How I used my smile to turn a bad situation around today:

_____

_____

_____

_____

_____

DATE: __ / __ / __

THE ROBBED THAT SMILES STEALS SOMETHING FROM THE THIEF.

William Shakespeare

How I used my smile to deflate a mean comment today:

_____

_____

_____

_____

_____

DATE: ___/___/___

Q: Is it right that your smile is insured?

JR: No ... If my smile was insured, there would be someone at my house on a nightly basis saying, "You need to floss longer."

Julia Roberts

What I do to maximize my smile (check all that apply):

- ☐ floss
- ☐ whiten
- ☐ apply lipstick
- ☐ meditate
- ☐ say "Cheese"
- ☐ _____
  other

Practice making a silly face, like Hokusai's hard-working actor:

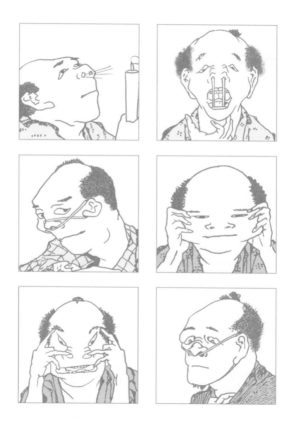

LOOK BACK AND SMILE ON PERILS PAST!

Sir Walter Scott

Today I looked back at this worry from the past and smiled:

_____

_____

_____

_____

_____

DATE: ___/___/___

EVEN IN YOUR DARKEST MOMENT, YOU USUALLY CAN FIND SOMETHING TO LAUGH ABOUT IF YOU TRY HARD ENOUGH.

Red Skelton

What I found to laugh away a dark moment today:

_____

_____

_____

_____

_____

DATE: __ / __ / __

DRAW A PROPER SMILE:

DATE: __ / __ / __

DRAW A SMIRKLE:

SMILE, I SAY, NOT SMIRKLE— MOUTH A SEMICIRCLE, THAT'S THE PROPER STYLE.

Lewis Carroll

A stale article, if you dip it in a good, warm, sunny smile, will go off better than a fresh one that you've scowled upon.

Nathaniel Hawthorne

Today I gave away an ☐ extra ☐ unused ☐ homemade ☐ small

_____ with a smile and enjoyed one in return.

DATE: ___/___/___

I HAVE WITNESSED THE SOFTENING OF THE HARDEST OF HEARTS BY A SIMPLE SMILE.

Goldie Hawn

I smiled at this hard heart today: _____ . What happened?

_____

_____

_____

_____

_____

Oh! It is only a novel! . . . only some work in which the most thorough knowledge of human nature, the happiest delineation of its varieties, the liveliest effusions of wit and humor are conveyed to the world in the best-chosen language.

Jane Austen

Author who always makes me smile:

_____

_____

_____

_____

_____

DATE: ___/___/___

that always **BOOKS** make me

SMILE

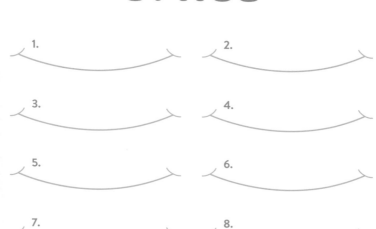

1.

2.

3.

4.

5.

6.

7.

8.

DATE: ___/___/___

There is nothing which has yet been contrived by man, by which so much happiness is produced as by a good tavern or inn.

Samuel Johnson

A good ☐ tavern ☐ inn ☐ bar ☐ coffee shop ☐ tea salon

☐ _____ where I smiled today:
　　　　　other

_____

_____

_____

_____

I DON'T KNOW THE SECRET OF HAPPINESS, BUT I'LL TELL YOU WHAT, I'VE NEVER BEEN SAD AT A MEXICAN RESTAURANT.

Unknown

A restaurant where I always feel happy:

_____

_____

_____

_____

_____

My way of joking is to tell the truth.

George Bernard Shaw

DATE: ___ /___ /___

SOMETHING TRUE ABOUT ME THAT MAKES OTHER PEOPLE SMILE:

_____

_____

_____

_____

_____

_____

DATE: ___ /___ /___

SOMETHING TRUE ABOUT ME THAT MAKES ME SMILE:

_____

_____

_____

_____

_____

_____

There's something you and I can give
  To others every day we live. . . .
It never costs us one thin dime
  Yet we can share it all the time.
The world is hungry for this gift
  That gives each weary one a lift.
A perfect touch, always in style:
  It's just a warm and friendly smile.

William Arthur Ward

A smile that lifted my sprits today:

_____

_____

_____

_____

_____

SMILE! IT INCREASES YOUR FACE VALUE!

Robert Harling

An event that increased my face value today:

_____

_____

_____

_____

_____

Pleasure is very seldom found where it is sought; our brightest blazes of gladness are commonly kindled by unexpected sparks.

Samuel Johnson

Something unexpected that sparked my smile today:

_____

_____

_____

_____

_____

DATE: ___/___/___

WHAT MADE ME SMILE TODAY · WHAT MADE ME SMILE TODA

Complete one or more prompts:

This surprise: _____

A walk to: _____

Looking at a photo of: _____

This comment: _____

This discount: _____

A long bath: _____

A fun new assignment: _____

Other: _____

COLORS ARE THE SMILES OF NATURE.

Leigh Hunt

My favorite colors in nature today:

_____

_____

_____

_____

_____

DATE: ___ / ___ / ___

What a desolate place would be a world without a flower! It would be a face without a smile, a feast without a welcome.

Clara Lucas Balfour

Flowers that made me smile today:

_____

_____

_____

_____

_____

DATE: ___/___/___

SOMETHING THAT MADE ME REALLY SMILE TODAY:

_____

_____

_____

_____

_____

_____

DATE: ___/___/___

A SMILE I GAVE JUST TO BE POLITE:

_____

_____

_____

_____

_____

_____

Her smile was as open as a small boy's, a personal enjoyment rather than a social gesture.

Mary Renault

I DO NOT NEED DRUGS TO BE A GENIUS . . . BUT I NEED YOUR SMILE TO BE HAPPY.

Charlie Chaplin

Sally has a smile I would accept as my last view of earth.

Wallace Stegner

_____ has a smile that I would accept as my last view on earth.

I want people to smile when they hear my name.

Lil B

When I hear these names I always smile:

_____

_____

_____

_____

_____

WORDPLAY

Girls' Names

**What could you name your daughter to make people smile?
Match the columns. (See answers below.)**

. . . if your last name is Turner? _____

. . . if your last name is Gardner? _____

. . . if your last name is Caine? _____

. . . if your last name is Dwyer? _____

. . . if your last name is Packer? _____

1. Fanny

2. Candy

3. Barb

4. Paige

5. Olive

Answers: 4, 5, 2, 3, 1

It takes 65 muscles to frown and 13 to make a smile. Why work overtime?

B. J. Palmer

How I saved 52 muscles today:

_____

_____

_____

_____

_____

SMILING IS MY FAVORITE EXERCISE.

Unknown

My smile "workout" for the day (a list of the things I smiled at or about):

_____

_____

_____

_____

_____

If you see
someone
without a
smile, give
them one of
yours.

Dolly Parton

DATE: ___/___/___

TODAY I GAVE MY SMILE TO _____ **, WHO LOOKED SAD. RESULT:**

_____

_____

_____

_____

_____

_____

DATE: ___/___/___

TODAY I GAVE MY SMILE TO _____ **, WHO LOOKED WORRIED. RESULT:**

_____

_____

_____

_____

_____

_____

SMILING IS A KIND OF MOUTH YOGA. WHEN WE SMILE, IT RELEASES THE TENSION IN OUR FACE.

Thich Nhat Hanh

How I felt after my "mouth yoga" practice today:

_____

_____

_____

_____

_____

_____

DATE: ___/___/___

Smile. It's the second-best thing you can do with your lips.

Jill Shalvis

The best thing I did with my lips today:

_____

_____

The best thing I smiled at today:

_____

_____

Draw an imaginary flower and give it a silly scientific name:

Name: _____

DATE: ___ / ___ / ___

Edward Lear imagined flowers and gave them scientific-sounding names, such as *Armchairia Comfortabilis* and *Crabbia Horrida* for these:

What did he call this specimen? (See answer below.)

Answer: *Manypeeplia Upsidownia*

Happiness is . . . finding two olives in your martini when you're hungry.

Johnny Carson

Happiness is _____

_____

_____

_____

_____

_____

I THINK CHEESE SMELLS FUNNY, BUT I FEEL BANANAS *ARE* FUNNY.

Joe Murray

Draw a food you think *is* funny:

DATE: ___/___/___

A WONDERFUL THOUGHT THAT MADE ME SMILE TODAY:

_____

_____

_____

_____

_____

_____

DATE: ___/___/___

A BEAUTIFUL MENTAL IMAGE THAT MADE ME SMILE TODAY:

_____

_____

_____

_____

_____